Why Are Th
What Can You
An Interac
Children, Parents, Counselors and Teachers

Written by Rich Linville
ISBN: 9781520496788

1. What do you think bullying is? Following each question are some possible answers. There can be other possible answers. You can pause now to think about or discuss this question: What is bullying?

1. Bullying is when a person says or does things to have power over others who are the targets. (Note: There are no guarantees about what works with bullies. What works with one bully; may not work with a different bully. Safety is first for everyone. Use common sense and think before you act. Most people are not bullies.)

Target of Bully   Bully

1. Bullying is when a person:
- says bad things to someone,
- does not let someone be part of a group,
- threatens someone,
- writes or says bad things about someone,
- ignores someone who's talking to them,
- makes someone feel scared or uncomfortable,
- hits or hurts someone
- takes or damages someone's things,
- makes someone do bad things that they don't want to do.
Can you think of other examples of bullying?
(You can pause now to think about or discuss this question.)

2. Why is someone a bully?
(You can pause now to think about or discuss this question.)

2. There are many reasons why someone might be a bully.
Here are some reasons:
- A bad home life may make someone a bully who wants to see others hurt and sad.
- Watching violent movies or games may cause a person to copy the movies or games.
- Because someone is mean to them, bullies may be unfairly mean to others.
- Lack of attention may cause a person to be a bully for attention.
- Being sad, hurt, or angry may make a person want to bully others.
- Sometimes there is no reason why people are bullies. They just are.

Can you think of other reasons why someone is a bully?
(You can pause now to think about or discuss this question.)

3. Who do you think might be the target of a bully?
(You can pause now to think about or discuss this question.)

3. Some people who might be targets of a bully are:

- People who have no friends may be a target of a bully.
- People who have a bad temper may be easily made angry by a bully who pushes their buttons.
- People who are bigger, smaller, larger, or thinner may be the target of a bully.
- People who have different skin color may be the targets of bullies.
- People who have handicaps may be targets of bullies.

Can you think of other reasons why someone may be the target of bullies?

(You can pause now to think about or discuss this question.)

See Something? Say Something!

4. Why do you think bullying is wrong?
(You can pause now to think about or discuss this question.)

4. There are many reasons why bullying is wrong. Here are some:

- Both bullies and targets of bullies may hurt themselves or others and become sad and lonely.
- Both bullies and targets of bullies may end up as school drop-outs and not get good jobs.
- Both bullies and targets of bullies may abuse drugs and ruin their health.
- Both bullies and targets of bullies may engage in fighting and be hurt or hurt others.

Can you think of other reasons that bullying is wrong?

(You can pause now to think about or discuss this question.)

5. If you do nothing about bullies, they may stay bullies and hurt you or someone else. What do you think a child can do about bullies and bullying? (You can pause now to think about or discuss this question.)

5. When it comes to bullies and bullying, a child can try these things:

- Don't be a bully. Be your best with everyone. Everyone has the right to be different. Be a buddy not a bully.
- Nobody is perfect but you are as good as anyone else.
- Always be on the look-out for bullies. Try to always be with people you trust or among a group of people that seem trustworthy.
- if a bully bothers you, scream loudly, look around you and run away to a safe adult or a place of safety.
- Don't say things to a bully unless you are well trained in talking to bullies. It can turn bad for you or others. Keep cool and later talk in private to a police officer or other responsible adults.

5. When it comes to bullies and bullying, a child can try these things:

- If you tell adults about bullying and nothing is done, tell other adults until something is done. Do not lie or exaggerate about what happened.
- If you see someone being bullied, either scream loudly and try to help the target by helping them get away or stand near them to show support by screaming at the bully. Always remember safety first for everyone.
- Don't try to fight a bully unless you are well-trained in self-defense. Even then a bully may have hidden weapons. Always be aware and careful around a bully.
- You can never know for sure what bullies will do. Be safe and carefully get away from bullies. Sooner or later many bullies end up in prison.

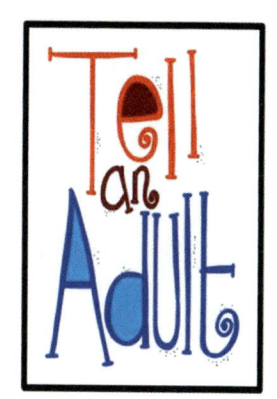

One of the best way to prepare for bullies and bullying is for you to act out or role-play in front of your mirror alone. In the mirror, look at your eyes and your body language. Show no fear. Also, you can privately practice in front of a responsible adult that you trust.

Here are some role plays for you to think about or discuss or with people you trust.

6. You are standing and a bully pushes you. What could you do? (You can pause now to think about or discuss this question.)

7. If you push back, a fight might start where you get hurt by one or more bullies. Use the pushing to keep you moving and run to a safe adult or a safe place.

8. You are eating and a bully throws food on you or knocks your food on the floor. What could you do?
(You can pause now to think about or discuss this question.)

8. Try not to cry because the bully wants you to cry. Don't throw food back because it might get out of hand and someone may get hurt. You might watch the bully out of the corner of your eye as you say nothing and quickly go away to find a police officer or other safe adult to help you deal with the bully. Your safety is more important than food.

9. A bully hits or threatens to hit you or someone else. What might you do? (You can pause now to think about or discuss this question.)

9. You might quickly look around for a place to go to and back away from the bully. If you know self-defense, be ready to use it. Be alert for other bullies around you with possible hidden weapons. Run to a safe adult or a safe place. Scream while you run.

10. Someone writes a bad note about you. What can you do next? (You can pause now to think about or discuss this question.)

10. Do not write a note back. It could be used against you. Save the note. If the note might be just a joke, you can ignore it by saying to yourself, "Words will NEVER hurt me." If it is a really bad note then save it and show it later to a safe adult. Don't throw away or tear up the note. Make several copies to keep as evidence. Put copies of the note in different places or give copies to many safe adults.

11. A bully is laughing at you and calling you names like, "You're stupid!", what might you do?
(You can pause now to think about or discuss this question.)

11. If you laugh at yourself, the bully might or might not stop bullying you. If you agree in a joking way with the bully by saying "Yes, I am!", the bully might or might not stop. If you call the bully names back, it might turn into a fight with you getting hurt. It's better to say nothing. Keep an eye on them as you walk or run away to a safe adult or a safe place.

12. You are alone. A group of bullies or one bully is picking on you, and threatening to hurt you if you tell anyone. Any ideas of what you could do? (You can pause now to think about or discuss this question.)

12. You might quickly look around for a place to go. Then, back away or run from the bully or bullies. If you know self-defense, be ready to use it. But still be alert for other bullies or hidden weapons.

13. Can you think of other role-playing questions and answers about bullies and bullying? (You can pause now to think about or discuss this question.)

14. What do you think an adult can do about bullies and bullying?
(You can pause now to think about or discuss this question.)

14. When it comes to bullies and bullying, an adult can try these things:

- Don't be an adult bully. Be your best with everyone. Everyone is different. Everyone has the right to be different but not the right to be a bully.
- Ask questions and talk with children and adults about bullies and bullying. To not talk about bullies and bullying is to make it worse. -
- Nobody is perfect but you are as good as anyone else.
- Always be on the look-out for a bully. Try to always travel with someone to help you. Don't be alone. Stand next to the target of a bully and offer help or say nice things to the target. Safely get away from the bully.
- Don't try to fight or say things to a bully unless you are well-trained in self-defense. The bully may have a hidden weapon. It can turn badly for you or others. Keep cool. Look for a safe place or safe adult to go to.

15. - If you tell the police, teachers, or other adults and they do nothing, keep talking to other responsible adults until something is done.

- Think before you act against a bully or bullies. Bullies or a bully may be dangerous to you and to others.

- Always be thinking about a safe place or safe adult. Scream and run to that safe place or safe adult.

- See something? Say something because bullies want you to say nothing.

See Something? Say Something!

16. - Try out for sports or practice self-defense. Don't force children to participate in an activity if they don't want to because there may be bullying going on in that activity. The parent should try to be at the activity as much as possible to watch out for bullying. There are self-defense classes near you, self-defense books and videos plus online books and online videos like You-Tube. Try to practice daily.

17. - From time to time, adults and children need to talk about what to do about bullies and bullying in order to take away any power bullies might try to have over their targets.
- Adults can role play with children for different situations of bullying.
"Knowledge is power."
- Francis Bacon
"None of us are as smart as all of us." - Kenneth H. Blanchard

Note to Kids, Parents, Teachers, Counselors and other Adults:

Thank you for purchasing this book. Illustrations purchased from Edu-Clips, OpenClipArt and Commons Wiki. For over 40 years, I have taught at elementary, high school and college levels. When I see bullying, I stand by the target if possible and intervene on behalf of the target with such comments to the bully as, "You're not that perfect to put down someone else." or "You don't have the right to hit someone." and "If you hit someone who disagrees with you, does that make you right?" or "Leave them alone. They have the right to be different and the right to a different opinion."

Thank you for your concern about what to do about bullying. To not talk about bullying and to look the other way is to support and embolden bullying.

I would love to hear from you. Email me at richardvlinville@gmail.com

Growth Mindset for Kids

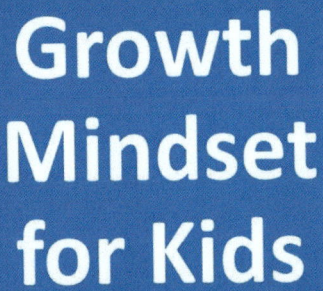

You also might like to read this book by Rich Linville

We All Have Brain Power!

Why do kids need to know about Growth Mindsets? Scientists have found that there are two different kinds of mindsets: FIXED MINDSETS and GROWTH MINDSETS. A fixed mindset never changes. In a Fixed Mindset your failures define you like, "I'm no good at dancing!" If I never learn new things or never make new friends, I have a fixed mindset. My growth mindsets can change! When I learn something new or challenging then I have a growth mindset like, "I can't dance yet. If I focus and practice, I can learn to dance."

Printed in Great Britain
by Amazon